ABOUT TIME

ABOUT TIME

poems by:

Neil Hilborn

Button Publishing Inc.

Minneapolis

2024

ABOUT TIME
POETRY
AUTHOR: Neil Hilborn
COVER DESIGN: Zoe Norvell

◇

◇

Published by Button Poetry
Minneapolis, MN 55418 | http://www.buttonpoetry.com

◇

Manufactured in the United States of America
PRINT ISBN: 978-1-63834-202-1
EBOOK ISBN: 978-1-63834-110-9
AUDIOBOOK ISBN: 978-1-63834-109-3

First printing

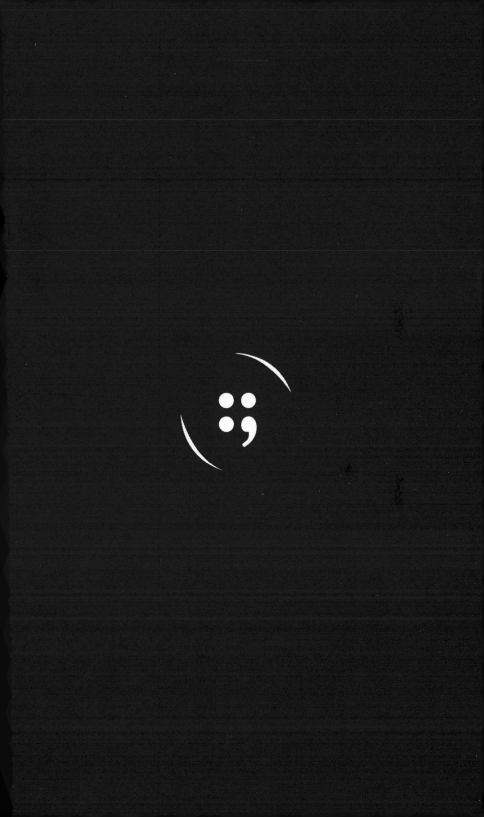

Anny, this book is for, because of, in support of, toward, around, and with love for, you.

CONTENTS

I

3   We Are Sitting in the Car after Leaving the Dog Park and Zoey, My Dog, Tells Me She Loves Me

5   Stop Me

7   First Impressions Practice

8   No Part

9   When I say that loving me is like a brick wall falling on your car in the parking lot of your own damn apartment complex

10   Able Was I Ere I Saw Des Moines

12   Combination 1432

13   The Holy Lance

14   Security Check

15   Cryoseism

17   Inside of Every Turducken is a Turd

18   Not Avoidant Just Tired

19   Zero

21   Rasp

22   Sevens Over Kings

24   Sven

26   The Vanishing Pharmacopeia (Or, Ballad for an Escape)

27   Personal Stuff Collage

28   Sean didn't want to go to the hospital because he had just turned 18 and was worried he'd be arrested, also he said he didn't have insurance because he thought it made him sound cool

30   Things I'm Gonna Lick Once COVID Is Over

31   Ekphrasis, Siberian Bear Hunting Armor, 1800s

32   Coroner's Voice Notes, July 5th, 2989, Neil Hilborn

33   Someone Asks Me After a Show How, If I Really Have OCD, I
      Can Shake Hands With Everyone in Line for Merch

II

37   A Wish for More Wishes

38   Satori

40   Alcoholism Screening Questionnaire

42   The Gulf Breeze Incident

43   A Long Night's Journey into Morning

45   Love Ends, but What If It Doesn't?

46   Photograph: The President's Box at Ford Theatre

47   Ugh Forgiveness

48   New Chemical

49   Florida Man Accused of Using Kool-Aid Packets to Steal Nearly
      $1,000 in Walmart Merchandise, a Requiem

50   Ekphrasis, Witches' Sabbath, Goya, 1798

51   Notes App Excerpt: Hormel Pepperoni Guy One Man Band Depression

53   The Difference Between Doing and Being

55   Soft Sentinel

56   Merging the Book Collections

57   Boggy Creek Must Be a Tributary of the Styx

58   The Stakes

59   Water Is Distantly Related to All Other Water

61   When I'm Allowed Out of My House Again, Assuming by then
      I've Got My Meds Figured Out, It's Over for You Bitches

63   Jackets

65   King of the Gods of Heaven and the Underworld

66   Raleigh in a Snow Globe

67   Opportunity, Wake Up!

III

71 About Every 75 Years

72 Sciurus vulgaris

74 My God, It's Full of Stars

76 Prayer to the Minor Deity of Left Turns

77 August 8th, 1969, Iain Macmillan Takes His Photograph of The Beatles Crossing the Street

78 I Hope You Dance (Until You Are Dead)

79 Waltz for a Doomed Relationship

81 The Nature of Nails

82 The Time a Kid Pulled a Knife on Me So I Pulled a Knife on Him

84 I put on my socks in the wrong order and now I'm gonna get hit by a car

85 The Earl Of

87 Deluge

89 A Third Place

91 Our Numbered Days

94 A Tirade Against Hot Tubs Giving Way to The Universal Consciousness

96 Ed White Elementary, Seabrook, Texas, Summer

98 Discarnate

99 Ekphrasis, Nighthawks, Edward Hopper, 1942

100 Hail the Fire and the Wall It Couldn't Bring Down

102 What I've Learned about Engines

104 Dick Shark

106 (I am large, I contain multitudes)

107 Hen Sonnet, or, Good Morning Ladies

108 Astros @ Cubs, June 10th, Night Game

110 December 21st, 2022, The Solstice

115   Liner Notes

119   About the Author

121   Author Book Recommendations

ABOUT TIME

I

Here's an odd and paradoxical truth: A man's experience of happiness can later kill him.

—Louise Erdrich

WE ARE SITTING IN THE CAR AFTER LEAVING THE DOG PARK AND ZOEY, MY DOG, TELLS ME SHE LOVES ME

I'm trying to do what my therapist recommended
and just sit in silence. The car isn't

running, the stereo isn't yelling
at me, nothing is happening at all

and sure, it's Saint Paul, Minnesota, where
shootings happen but not in whatever

neighborhood one happens to be in,
and it's just gotten dark and no one

on this or any adjacent street has started
their cars in like a month, quarantine

you know, and I'm trying to sit in abject
silence for like three fucking minutes

but the ringing in my ears has become
a bell and then a conspiracy of bells

and then whatever sound comes thirty seconds after
a pipe bomb and my brain is shouting

over the top of it I am going to kill myself
I am going to kill myself and I, me, not

the voice which sounds like me but isn't me,
I try to think of what my therapist, whose name

is Erin, Erin, I remind myself, told me:
acknowledge the thoughts but don't

attach to them; pay attention to your hands
and what around you they can touch; notice

your breathing, I know it's corny but do it,
notice the way your shirt touches
somewhere new as your breath

moves you; ask the thoughts what
they want: why am I going to

kill myself and if I do, go all the way
to the logical end: who will it hurt,

what gets left behind, what good remains
undone; dissect the bells, separate

the ringing into a flat expanse
and not the towering blaze it's telling you

it is, what does each bell sound like
and who carried them there and when

will they be called away—notice
your hands your fucking hands—

which is when Zoey, my dog, who I love,
who came to us six months ago

from a house that tried and failed
to love her, licks my ear. She's right,

we've been sitting here too long. I start
the car and let it warm up for a minute

because it looks like it might snow.

STOP ME

Stop me if you've heard this one: a guy
walks into a bar and says Take my wife, please,
she deserves to be happy. A guy walks
into a bar and asks for a sandwich. The bartender
says We don't serve food here. The guy says
Then I stole someone's sandwich
last time I was here. Stop me
if you've heard this one: a guy
walks into a bar for the fifth time
this week and it's Thursday. A guy
walks into a bar, is greeted by the bartender
and two regulars, and he does not
turn around. A guy walks into
a bar because outside it's a whole bunch
of stuff that's not the bar
and inside it's just the bar. A guy
walks into his living room because
all the bars are closed. A guy reaches
all the way back in the liquor cabinet
because he wouldn't appreciate
the good stuff right now. Stop me
if you've heard this one. A guy walks
into a bar and keeps walking. A guy
puts a twenty into the juke box even though
no one asked him to. A guy is dancing
alone even though the bar is not empty.
A guy gets on a train but the train
has a bar. A guy goes for a walk
by the train tracks but someone clearly
last night turned that into a bar. A guy
walks into the bar with a joint and says
Hey what kind of joint is this. A guy lights
a joint but he's outside the bar, by
himself and the dumpster. A guy writes
on the dumpster Help please.

A guy is always seeking aid
in ways that can be mistaken
for a good time. A guy is handshakes
with no eye contact. Fireworks
at 3 PM. Snow angels before
the blizzard ends. A guy walks
into a bar and for the first time this week
for like thirty minutes he feels good
about himself. It's Thursday.

FIRST IMPRESSIONS PRACTICE

Hi hello my name is Neil and I hope
you like poems about poems about mommy
issues and slowly losing your mind,
because I was raised wrong and I am very
crazy. I'm like if Caligula had no power
and a credit card spending limit. I'm Captain
Ahab without all the chill vibes. I'm the fly
that can't remember the way it got in
your house, which is to say that I am
constantly smashing myself into everything
that looks like a way out, which is
to say that the first thing I do in any room
is figure out how to leave, which is to
say hi hello, I'm so honored you invited
me to your party, I'm sorry I can't stay.

NO PART

Everything I ever asked for, I received. Advantages
and punishments. Shots and bars. Songs

inside the fog inside the world. Take it
from me, it's possible to ask for the wrong

things. I said I wanted crazy love and I got
it. I asked for an accurate mirror and pain

is what I received. I thought that it would
be interesting to be sad and you know

what, I was right. Sadness drifted
into the apartment and made sure

we'd always remember its visit. Blue hair

in every drain. New butt prints in the couch,
its name carved into all the food in the fridge.

I am a long drive to a closed restaurant. I'm a mistake
everyone has to pretend was intentional.

I'm a fist full of electricity: some nights
I walk in the house and all the lightbulbs explode.

WHEN I SAY THAT LOVING ME IS LIKE A BRICK WALL FALLING ON YOUR CAR IN THE PARKING LOT OF YOUR OWN DAMN APARTMENT COMPLEX

after Hanif Abdurraqib

what I mean is that you know you shouldn't have parked there; the wall has been leaning suspiciously for a while like a drunk in a steady wind. The wall has never had good posture but lately it's been slouching as though someone asked it to solve for X. The weather has been bad so that usually makes the wall more unstable. Bad weather includes heat, cold, no rain, all clouds, all wind, all teeth. What I mean is that even though you have insurance the whole thing is gonna be a pain in the neck to explain. Like, a wall? A thing that is supposed to just stand there? Did you do anything to the wall? Oh, you just relied on it to do its one and only job? City records indicate that it's not technically your wall and therefore its fortification isn't your responsibility, but the wall's keeper is aloof and refuses to be reached by email. The wall's keeper was a wall maintainer in the early 2000s but since then a lot of shit has happened. Maybe you should have insisted someone reinforce the wall with Lexapro or weed. Maybe if you hadn't been around its collapse wouldn't have been a big deal and it could have calmly adapted to its new life as the ground. The only difference between waking and sleeping is your relationship to the horizon. If you're laying down you're always asleep. There are ways to be vertical and accomplish nothing. The wall would dream about you if it could.

ABLE WAS I ERE I SAW DES MOINES

Putting aside, for a second, reality, let's agree
that the weather in Des Moines is always grey
and 62. The clouds over Des Moines
are always spelling out your name. Not your name
like the thing you tell people to call you, your Name,
your True Name, the way you address yourself
in empty rooms, the sound the beast makes
every night before it lunges at you. The clouds
in Des Moines know that. Des Moines has
been waiting for you like a taxi at a midnight
airport. The escape hatch once all the other doors
have slammed shut. You call it a talisman
but that's a fancy way of saying security
blanket. If everything goes to shit,
maybe because of an accident but probably
because you make bad decisions, you can always
go to Des Moines. Be a dishwasher
and start drinking again. Why go to another
bar when you get off when you're already
at a bar; work smarter not harder. So in
Des Moines the weather is unchanging
and mediocre because Des Moines is
stasis. A Midwestern city about which no one
has anything bad to say. There are things to hate
about Omaha and Peoria, but Des Moines is all
four apartments over a pizza place. Des Moines
is Targets next to Home Depots and folks
visiting their folks every Sunday for dinner.
Des Moines is where you think you could go
so no one will ever again expect anything
from you. In Des Moines you can do whatever
you want as long as what you want is to sit
in a dark room with your hand moving toward
and away from your mouth. You cradle
Des Moines inside yourself like some people

keep one bullet chambered in their gun.
Des Moines is where nothing has to mean
anything anymore. In Des Moines it's always
grey and 62. In Des Moines the clouds know
your name, your true name; you can run
as far as you want, you can cut your hair
and change your accent, and when you get to
Des Moines you'll fuck it all up again. The beast
leaps out of the dark and offers you its claws.

COMBINATION 1432

My brother opens his gun safe
and hands me a pistol. Because
this is the first time I've been back
to Texas since he and my dad
really got into guns, I handle
it like a dang liberal, both hands,
fingers extended, black aperture
pointed toward the floor. The safe
thunks closed and he stands up with
what then I'd call a cowboy
rifle cradled in the crook
of his arm. Now I'd call it a 30/30
Winchester, as though knowledge
makes a thing less deadly or
as though when we were kids
he didn't chase me through
the house with a kitchen knife.
My brother hands me a gun and
a case for it, and he says,
"Cool, let's go."

THE HOLY LANCE

The most miscreant thing I ever did
was at my friend Evan's Catholic day
camp. It was just one of those things,
I slept over at his house Saturday night,
which I knew was a trap because Sunday
was for the Lord or whatever, but I figured
that the one time I read Nietzsche
would inoculate me. Tiny, crunchy heathen
that I was, I did not know there were so many
songs about Jesus. You could fill an iPod nano
with all the songs about the Christ
we sang facing one another
in a circle. They sang, I mouthed
the word "watermelon" because that
looks like most syllables. It was lunch
time for the third time and all I had
left was the big sassy orange my mom packed
me, huge, stupid, falling apart orange
that represented our family: overripe, finished
already, only held together by inertia.
Lunch was in the gym, big Catholic carpeted
gym over which loomed big bleeding
Catholic Jesus. Bone white Jesus on a bone
white cross. Pale green of the stained glass.
Pale green of the carpet. I hated Jesus
just as much as my family so I hucked
the orange at his dumb dead wizard face,
but eleven-year-olds can't throw that far so
instead of becoming Saint Longinus
I became a kid who threw an orange
at a girl for no reason. She was weeping
because you would too if an orange exploded
in your face. I never learned her name; I was
already being dragged by my arm toward the car.

SECURITY CHECK

What's your least favorite city? Did you fly

or drive there? When the guy took your

wallet, did he have a gun or just a hand

in a jacket pocket? In which sock did

you hide your cash? If you could go back

ten hours, would you? If you travel back in time

to kill your grandfather, do you cease to exist

or were you always supposed to kill him? Where

do you go when you need to hide? Is it

your sock? Is it gone forever? Who do you

go home to? Who have you made guilty? What

has somebody told you not to tell? Do you

hope you won't be found out? Did you

come to Earth for evil purposes? If

given the chance, would you exchange your life

for a new one? How about now? How about now?

CRYOSEISM

Ok so let's say The Bloop
actually is glaciers splitting.
That's good, right? I know
it's bad and I know glaciers

can't reproduce, much less
sexually, but more glaciers

can't be bad, right? Oh

what's that? We want like
two or three really big ones?
Well I've got an ice maker,
could that help? I know

getting my ice to the glaciers
could be a problem but like

what if I drove

to way northern Canada
with my A/C all the way
up? You don't have to tell me
I'm dumb, I know I'm dumb,

I just wanna help and all
the non-ridiculous things

I've been trying don't seem

to have done shit, so next time
instead of washing the pasta sauce
out of another fucking glass
jar to go in the fucking

recycling or bringing my stupid
little bag to the grocery store I'm gonna

pack my car with ice and start driving.

INSIDE OF EVERY TURDUCKEN IS A TURD

Hey what's up you wanna have a medium plus night at a barcade that ends in two hours of foreplay with absolutely no orgasms? Well then come on down to Dating Neil at 22-Years-Old-World. We've got happy hours at the only bar in Minnesota that doesn't have a bathroom. We've got bike rides not for fun but because he doesn't have a car. We've got his roommate playing Madden 2006 (even though it's 2012!) right outside the door while you do foreplay for two hours! It goes cunnilingus immediately, then talking because he's scared, then a hand job, then sleep. And just look at him: he's everything you'd hope an early 20s part-manimal hipster might be: he's got on suspenders and a v neck so low you can see his navel; he works at a shoe store and he'll tell you to come in during his shift so he can touch your feet while he puts shoes on you, which neither of you will like; he only just discovered his beard connects below his mutton chops and he is clinging to those 45 hairs. He's like if a pigeon didn't shower. He's got chewed-up fingernails and real long toenails. He's what a Smashing Pumpkins song smells like. He's like a teddy bear covered in tomato sauce sitting in a gutter: even if you take him home, clean him off, and love him with everything you have, he will not, under any circumstances, comfort you.

NOT AVOIDANT JUST TIRED

I have no interest today in being vulnerable.
I went outside, to the grocery store
even, and I made eye contact with upwards
of two people. I made the correct gestures
to appear human, I did all the standard
sounds with my mouth, so I would like
full credit for being seen today,
please. I'm a flim-flam machine
that turns sadness into money and money
into sandwiches. The sandwiches are fuel
for road trips toward you guessed it
sadness. Since I went to therapy yesterday
and today I just cannot feel *exposed*, here
is a list of things I like: sandwiches, and I know
I just said sandwiches make me sad
but sandwiches are large and contain
multitudes; the beginnings of movies; the way
my breath fogs the car windows before
it's warm; new vines at night; damaged
wood finish; sparks from trailer chains
dragging down the highway; more time
before you have to leave; the flat expanse
of Iowa; the start of the day and how it does
not follow the end; how nothing ever really ends.

ZERO

0.

The first time I was aware
that humans wanted to kill
each other was a news segment
recapping the first Gulf War.
I was maybe seven and through
night vision goggles the missiles
looked like paper planes
meandering away. No explosions,
no bodies, no proof of where they went.

0.

I eat sunflower seeds every day,
but now I eat them harder and faster.

0.

Tsar Nicholas II orders his troops
to fire on protesters demanding
bread. A few days later bullets
are ricocheting off the gem stones
sewed into the lining
of his children's clothes.
Bulletproof vests
made of pressure and time.

0.

I watch a TikTok of a nuclear physicist
describing how best to avoid atomic
fallout. Basically, if you don't die
immediately, stay in your basement

for a couple weeks. The plume
can't find you if you hide from it.

0.

The Doomsday Clock has always
felt like a thing I made up. Like I was
trying to explain to my therapist that
I'm always relatively close to
killing myself, but there are still many
steps between me and the bridge.
The Doomsday Clock started at seven
seconds to midnight. Right now
it's at one hundred.

0.

On my first birthday Iraq invades
Kuwait. Burning oil wells, one candle.

0.

Napoleon enters Russia with thin
coats and unlined boots. Putin
enters Ukraine with not enough
bread or diesel. There's no such
thing as bad weather, only
inadequate clothes.

RASP

I have decided that I will no longer be mad
at my mother for not vaccinating me as a child.

I'll still be mad for a while but I will try not to be.
I have decided that instead of my persistent

cough being due to a teenage case of pertussis,
it's because a fir tree is growing in my lungs.

That happened once to a man in Russia. I've never
been to Russia but it's nice to think that I am a place

where something could blossom. Something did grow
in me, I guess, a virus, but viruses don't grow

they just become more. A virus found in me
an open door and drew itself in every picture

frame. A virus propped open all the windows.
It left all the floors clean in the way that dust

doesn't collect in wind tunnels. A beach scraped
bare after a hurricane. Tornado alley

and Chicago sidewalks. A tree is growing inside me
because otherwise I'm in pain for no reason. Better

to be flowers growing around a grave than a bouquet
in a vase.

SEVENS OVER KINGS

To quote my favorite TV personality
slash parasocial therapist slash
mommy? Doctor Robin Zasio of *Hoarders*
fame: you've got to feel it
to heal it. As it relates to hoarding I think
she means that if you never
throw out the things you accumulate then
you don't have to deal with
the emotional context around those things.
You stack newspapers
on top of the one containing your father's
obituary. Once the baby toys
have gathered enough dust you can't
tell which ones used to
be yours. I don't have a collection of anything
except maybe shoes with clean
soles and gifts I'd give people if I could manage
to see them if I could manage
to text them back, but I think I understand
what it feels like to pile up
nonsense until you no longer have to deal
with yourself. My heart
is a bedroom filled to the ceiling
with clothes. My heart is so
full, like acid reflux, like the lake is all
the way up its banks
and a storm is coming, full like a dumpster
outside a condemned daycare,
and if you've got to feel it to fuckin heal it,
then here goes: I have thought
about killing myself every thirty seconds
for the last twenty years.
I'm only sure I'm awake when I think
about it because in my dreams
I never once want to die. I don't say it much

because I don't really have time
to go to the beige hospital with no shoelaces,
and anyway if I was going to
do it I think I would have by now, but that doesn't
mean it's not always there,
the wall that gives me shade even as I try
to pull it down. The way out,
fitted with a padlock and chain. I'm so full
that every part of me
is now structurally integral. Remove
any brick and the whole
house will explode.

SVEN

The goblin assigned to ruin my life
has been getting better at his job.
The shadowy organization dishing out
edicts was unhappy with his
performance—I got married, I hadn't
smashed my head into anything
in a while, I wasn't sad about my dad
all the time—so the goblin had to get
devious. I imagine his name is Sven
and his favorite snack is peppermints
dipped in orange juice. Sven drives
a Toyota Celica in ostrich-dropping
yellow. Sven tells you he found a hilarious
television show, you have to come over
and watch it, and then he hands you
unsalted cashews and turns on
Friends. Sven saw that
most of the things I liked involved leaving
my house, so he figured out a way to
punish me for being comfortable out
in the world. I'm not deluded
or egotistical enough to believe in Conspiracy
Theories. The moon isn't a hologram
and the trails behind planes are fuckin steam.
But I'm starting to see how it would be
comforting to think that someone out there
has a plan. Not only do they have a plan,
but that plan is working. It's working so well
that now I have to stay inside where the liquor
is. See, that was Sven's plot all along, to get me
in the house at midnight with a fifth
of Jameson and no plane to get on
in the morning. Sven saw that I was feeling
like my life had purpose and he figured out

a way to rid the world of purpose. The whiskey
makes it easier to do stuff but it also
makes doing nothing bearable. The whiskey
stretches thirty seconds of joy into half
an hour. The easiest thing in the world
is to keep drinking the whiskey, and what I
have to remember are the reasons not to start.

THE VANISHING PHARMACOPEIA
(OR, BALLAD FOR AN ESCAPE)

This one, the new psychiatrist says,
is gonna be magic. And here's the thing—
I believe her, or I'm willing to; I want to
be better and I'm willing to believe
that this is part of how to get better.
Cause see the Lexapro made me
tired. The Abilify made me tired. The Prozac
makes me less tired but I'm still pretty
tired but maybe that's cause depression
makes you tired. Anyway I've just finished
downplaying my intrusive thoughts
about suicide to my new psychiatrist
—they're not that bad, sure they're every day
but I don't have a plan or anything—and she
tells me Lamictal is magic. I'm ready
to believe in magic. Give me an elephant
and all the right mirrors. Give me a bullet
suddenly cradled in the palm. Something has to
disappear, please let it not be me.

PERSONAL STUFF COLLAGE

Here is what I think it is good to know: I was born
somewhere and then I left. Somewhere is Texas,

now I'm gone. We lived in a house that dove
underwater three times. Three new sets of carpet,

all the furniture stacked on the beds and counters.
All the windows boarded up with no guarantee

of when light would arrive again. The first time
I drove a car I ran into a stop sign. No one saw

so I just drove away. For years the sign flirted
with the ground until one day, in the heat,

it collapsed. The damage we do keeps unfolding
even after we are gone. The first time I kissed

a boy was at the *Rocky Horror Picture Show*
under the screen with the spotlight on me

and someone else's hand on the back of my head,
and the second time was later that night in the dark

with no one watching or deciding anything
for me. My black lipstick, the rice and toilet paper

arcing across the sky. I've had seven concussions
that I'll list now: bicycle accident thrown rock

fencing mishap circle pit stage dive fight
in parking lot bicycle accident. There are ways

to harm yourself and make it look like you're having fun.

SEAN DIDN'T WANT TO GO TO THE HOSPITAL BECAUSE HE HAD JUST TURNED 18 AND WAS WORRIED HE'D BE ARRESTED, ALSO HE SAID HE DIDN'T HAVE INSURANCE BECAUSE HE THOUGHT IT MADE HIM SOUND COOL

It's Christmas Eve and there haven't been any shows for a week, so what are a bunch of suburban punks supposed to do except drive around in Joey's busted Crown Vic and cause light criminal mischief? We've decided that the new trend of inflatable Christmas ornaments is an affront to us since we all vocally don't believe in God and we say we hate Capitalism, though we're not clear on what the alternative would be. Sean has his dad's "old" army folding knife that looks brand new, no combat, never even opened quickly, and he sprints out of the passenger seat to slash Santa's throat. Santa collapses into a pool of no blood as Rudolph falls beside him. Sean makes it back to the car before the Hatebreed song ends the way every single Hatebreed song ends. Two houses down there's a Nativity scene and we've prepared for this. I crouch through the shadows because the family is inside watching The Grinch, no shit, arrayed there on the couch and stairs while I Grinch it up on their lawn. The Grinch, no shit; some things you make up for poems because they sound good and some things really just happened. I creep through the spotted darkness and replace the baby Jesus with a potato. I have a whole sack of potatoes. I said I came prepared. Some of the Jesuses were plastically part of the mangers in which they slept, so the potatoes land wherever they can: in place of a donkey, stuck on a wise man's staff, anywhere that said, "Lol you believe in god lol so dumb." Eventually every Frosty the Blow-Up Man has been murdered and every pastoral miracle disturbed, so Sean suggests that we drive by Jamie's house. Jamie and Sean just broke up, which I know but Joey doesn't because Jamie and I work together at the Worst Subway in Texas, a job from which I'm about to be pretty much fired for eating a foot long sandwich every two hours instead of my allotted six inch every four. Joey senses the gravity of the situation so he creeps down Jamie's street and there it is, her Scion xB, nicknamed The Toaster like every single other Scion xB.

Sean opens the door slowly, flips open the Santa Slayer, and this idiot, this dumb motherfucker, *stabs* the rear tire. It's called slashing tires for a reason. His hand slipped up the blade and suddenly his index, middle, and ring finger are pouring out their red lesson onto the Houston asphalt. Sean didn't want to go to the hospital because he had just turned 18 and was worried he'd be arrested, also he said he didn't have insurance because he thought it made him sound cool, but Joey and I know he's lying because he whipped out his USAA card after that guy in Tripp pants knocked his tooth out at the Napalm Death show. It's easier to give something up than call your friend a liar so I wrap Sean's hand in my Comeback Kid shirt. I know my mom will be asleep when I get home because by then she'd already been sick for a few years. I'm right: the only lights on are the porch and the kitchen. I am king, barbarian, shirtless, not covered in blood but spattered, about to be 17.

THINGS I'M GONNA LICK ONCE COVID IS OVER

Handrails and elevator buttons. Your mom
haha. I'm gonna sit outside ice cream
parlors, scare children so they drop
their cones, then I'm gonna clean plate club
the sidewalk. When the hand sanitizer
smells good I'm gonna find out
if it tastes good too. I'm gonna greet
everyone with a firm handshake
and a tongue to the eyeball. Hey world,
it's yer boy Neil, who wanna kiss.

EKPHRASIS, SIBERIAN BEAR HUNTING ARMOR, 1800s

I need you to know that I am not lying
when I say it's a suit of leather armor
covered in three-inch spikes accompanied
by, and this is the creepiest part, a full-face
helmet, also with spikes. Spikes on the damn
taint and eyelids. No spikes on the neck,
which seems like an oversight to me,
but I'm not a bear hunter so. Like everything
too rad to live (dinosaurs, dunkaroos) the bear
armor is probably a hoax put there by God
to test our faith, but that didn't stop me
and my more straight edge friends
from driving the hour and a half between our part
of Houston to the main part of Houston
to hang out with the Spiky Man
every other weekend. Sure they were
there for the Rothko Chapel or the Warhol
Soup Can, which were objectively the correct
choices, but the only right things in my life
were the ones that chose me so fuck it,
Spiky Man forever. I hope that the next time
I start my fourth spin of an album I don't like
I remember you, looming there among
all that meaning. Praise upon Spiky
Man and his refusal to be pretty in a world
that wants it. Thank you, Spiky Man.
Long after we are dead may you be
punching bears in heaven.

Jenny, when you said we were getting an early cyborg, I didn't think you meant version 0.1. I think I'm remaining within the bounds of dispassionate observation when I say that this guy is fucked up. He's got extra hands, just, on his elbows? Not even chest hands, elbow hands. He's got one of those discontinued transparent throat modules. Some of his Orichalcum parts have laser etched tattoos, but not...well done? Like maybe he did them himself? Perhaps he missed having a crawfish on his ankle. Must have been lonely for a pre-alpha organo-synth. Anyway, he left us a note in this pocket in his knee. I'm certain it's to us because it starts, "Dear autopsy person, earth-bound or otherwise. This is my body. It was made wrong to begin with and I saw no need to ever make it right. Please find in it the reason for my death (spaceship accident) as well as my favorite ways to waste my time. There was going to the grocery store a lot. There was podcasts while walking quickly through the woods. There were experimental stunt spaceships, but you knew about that. Please find also my sincerest hope that there's something in here you can use. Some cog or flywheel not manufactured since the 2300s. Maybe someone's knees have been clicking for a few centuries and now they don't have to anymore. I had so much of this life, please help me give some of it away."

SOMEONE ASKS ME AFTER A SHOW HOW, IF I REALLY HAVE OCD, I CAN SHAKE HANDS WITH EVERYONE IN LINE FOR MERCH

First of all, it seems insane now that I would
willingly shake hands with hundreds of strangers
in a bar in Tampa, Florida, but it was 2019
and COVID was still jokes I read on the internet.
Actually, no, really first of all fuck you, I spent so much
money and goddamn time just so I could use my hands
to greet people. In fact I am losing my whole entire
shit right now. I won't be ok until about two
AM when the adrenaline switches off and I pass out
in the hotel room, but for now the Jameson and half
a toke are keeping the voices in check so that I can
greet y'all like a fuckin American, right foot planted,
left foot back, smile on my face, hand lightly resting
on your shoulder if I know you, and I'm sorry
that I'm not as fucked up as you imagined I'd be,
really actually I'm sorry, because here's the thing
I feel weird saying: my mental illness paid for me
to treat my mental illness. That's a reductive way to talk
about it but I'm mad so here goes: you paid 20 bucks
to watch someone be crazy professionally, and I can see
why you'd be disappointed that I've only got some
misfiring cylinders and that I'm not rusting in some
junkyard, but a side effect of not giving my skull
an open floor plan is that I can now say hello
with more than just my voice, so here we are. Hi,
my name is Neil, thanks so much,
you fucker, for being here.

II

I was much further out than you thought
And not waving but drowning.

—Stevie Smith

A WISH FOR MORE WISHES

Here's another thing about which I was wrong:
I used to be certain that, in the event
of a zombie apocalypse, my anxiety would suddenly
go away. My paranoia would be an asset because
ineffable dark forces actually would be out
to get me. I wouldn't have uncertainties
about my job because my only occupation
would be: get food, kill zombie. Of course I know
enough about being mentally ill to know
that the zombies are just a metaphor for any
cataclysmic shift. It's just nice to imagine a world
in which the exhausting parade of choices
is pared down. I can't decide which baristas
to avoid because none of the coffee shops are there
anymore. You see where I'm going with this.
Only things to do in a cage are sleep and eat
when the door pops open. Your plane waiting
on the tarmac for a year and a half. I once thought
it would be ideal to decide three things
a day, and then the severed paw curled a finger
and, when asked do I want to eat, send
emails, or go for a stupid little walk, my answer
was always sleep. So when the zombies come,
I'll be the one in the middle of the street
yelling at the sky. Because I don't think I could
take it. I know something new about myself:
when I most needed to be solid, I crumbled
and stayed in pieces. When the zombies
come, for the little while the cell phone towers
are still working, don't call me. I'll already be gone.

SATORI

It used to be that my only shot
at enlightenment was biking
in traffic. Something about keeping
pace with a car for long enough
to make eye contact with the
passenger. Weaving around
parked cars while keeping their
doors closed through mere
willpower, something about digging
into my legs and extracting
enough power to *go*
could drag me toward a reverie
in which I was never anxious, never
had been, where I could be alive
without feeling the towering weight
of having to live. Then I acquainted
my head with asphalt in a rapid,
unsafe manner, and the doctor
told me that I could continue
either getting concussions or knowing
how to read, so. The bicycle lives
in the basement now and its tires
are sad. It's not rusted yet but
it will be soon; this is the part
where I'm supposed to say that now
I've got something just as good,
that I've found a new way
to find myself, but I haven't.
The stationary bike is fine
but it's just that: stationary. Being
on stage is better but I don't get to
do that without at least a car, a highway,
and probably an airplane involved. My
brain is too shitty for yoga and I like

my neighbors too much to take up
the drums, so what's a boy to do
when he found Elysium but had to
walk away? Am I allowed more than one
oasis? What's the word for continuing
to love the thing that tried to kill you?

ALCOHOLISM SCREENING QUESTIONNAIRE

Have you ever felt that you ought to cut down on your drinking?

> Always more fun in beginnings than
> endings. Every show abandoned
> halfway through the last season.
> Every pizza with a slice left for
> whatever might be hungry. Every
> drink though, every drink consumed.

Have you ever had a drink first thing in the morning to steady your nerves or get rid of a hangover?

> That's just Cancún baby. And while
> Cancún is Cancún, so are
> Minneapolis and Saint Paul.
> Christmas is Cancún. Wednesday,
> camping trips, just got fired, all
> Cancún.

Are you taking this test for yourself or someone else?

> The booze is so I don't have to
> confront myself, so the one I'm
> taking this for is me. I'm fucked up.
> Not a friend, me.

What is your age?

> I've got a pretty solid data sample by
> now. Enough points that a graph is
> starting to appear. Hard to refute the
> evidence when it begins to form a
> pile.

Have you ever felt that you ought to cut down on your drinking?

How easy it would be to go until I'm
forced to stop. To say I burned the
house down because I wanted to live
in the ashes. If decisions are scary,
remove them. Let the choice be a
cold glass of no choice at all. Elixir
of the last night in town. Tonic of I'll
sleep anywhere.

THE GULF BREEZE INCIDENT

"In sleep you know" is what the aliens said to Ed Walters
on that November night in 1988. The air in the Florida
panhandle is still too thick and slow to be air. Ed is trying
to breathe soup as the sun settles on him and his malfunctioning
pool pump. The familiar hum begins. The blue light
descends, just like in the movies, and you can say
it's because of the movies if you want to, but no matter
how right you probably are, I'd rather live in a world I don't
fully understand. So the Greys have come back for Ed
and he's shouting into the probably empty sky, "What
do you want from me!?" The only response: "In sleep
you know." Ed dreams of two snakes coiling
around a severed arm. A child crying at the end
of a hallway lined with chairs. He's mowing his lawn
with a razor blade. He's watching himself watch himself
sleep. Ed wakes and doesn't know shit. Goddamn aliens
and their goddamn promises. Ed fries eggs for breakfast.
Ed loads his gun. The next time that blue light barges
in Ed waves the pistol at the sky and demands to know what
he doesn't know. No answer this time, just the hum fading
toward dawn like a moving truck containing your best
friend. Ask the emptiness a question and receive
emptiness in return. Spend your days waiting for sleep.
In sleep you know, and the morning burns it all away.

A LONG NIGHT'S JOURNEY INTO MORNING

I need to talk about the head injury
I received in 2012. That was the November
that I fell through as though I were a comet

caught in Jupiter's inevitable arms.

There are things to say about my broken
bicycle and helmet, the mugging
that got me there, the snow falling

while the kids went through my pockets.

I need to process those things too,
but not here. Here I want to say
that the hospital was surprisingly

warm. The nurses charged my phone

so I could call Hieu and Sarah, who were
waiting for me at my house. It was still
snowing when they released us all

at four AM with instructions to not let me
sleep for a while. Warm like the hospital
was the Perkins where I ate pancakes

and watched the sun come up

over University Avenue. The pancakes
were the boat and the syrup the river.
The pancake boat of Charon and the syrup

River Styx. The river through Asphodel,

warm like the hospital, the boat, the pancake
boat that led me through that unimaginable
night into the tedious day. The day melts

snow and allows robot phone calls. The day

of alarms and bus schedules. The day I
never asked for but nonetheless received.
The day came and into its light I emerged

a more fearful person, all broken shoulder

and not going out alone to greet the street
lamps. Not all hard times turn you
into a better person. Sometimes you go

through something that undoes

all the work you did before, all the
yoga and therapy and "being mindful,"
all that good shit just falls apart

like a broken wheel, spokes leaping
into the darkened row of hedges. Sometimes
you're in pain, but you don't learn a thing.

LOVE ENDS, BUT WHAT IF IT DOESN'T?

after Ada Limón

Say, for instance, that love only ends
for one person at a time. No one has ever said
the sentence, "Hey I'm getting the vibe
that overnight we both fell out of love,
right?" One is always disappointed
by either leaving or death, which I guess is
just a more permanent kind of leaving.
Love is a cracked sidewalk the city will
never get around to fixing. Love is a perfect
rock on a beach filled with perfect rocks. Love
gets here when it's good and prepared and leaves
before the party even starts to wind down.
I have asked love to end and it said I wasn't
ready. Goddamn, I wept to my mom about
how I wished I didn't love someone undeserving
and even through that indignity my heart
held on. Stupid heart, no map and still believing
it knows the way. Dumb heart and its dumb need
to leap at what might knock it flat. If love
doesn't end then will some part of me remain
on that couch crying to mom forever? That was
the first couch I ever owned. It was beige
and hideous and I found it on a curb but it was
mine. My mustard stains and tears. My hours
sweating when the need to not be seen
was greater than the need to find AC. My love,
dwindling slowly but never disappearing.
Love ends, it had better.

PHOTOGRAPH: THE PRESIDENT'S BOX AT FORD THEATRE

Lincoln loved theatre, I hear. That's theatre with an RE. ER theater wouldn't be invented until 1995 by George Clooney's haircut. The box was two boxes with a movable wall in between in case something needed to be suddenly made larger. In the photograph the wall is at rest. Nothing yet is wrong.

UGH FORGIVENESS

I've been holding on to this anger
at my mom for so long that it feels

like without it I might disappear.
It's easier to just stay mad than forgive

her, in the same way that when food
burns my hands I throw it in my mouth.

If I don't stop moving no flies will
have time to land on me. If I don't stop

to breathe I can never truly know
if I'm choking. If I put on my coat first

then you have to wait until after
I leave. I say goodnight when it's only

dusk. I didn't have to
hang up first, but I did.

NEW CHEMICAL

I know why, but why is it that the pills

will keep me alive but they give me enough
to kill myself? Obviously it's not one

to one; I don't take the pills and then just

continue living, but they do make me want
to continue to get sandwiches

and repaint the living room instead of find

the edge of the coil. So I'll take the poison
in small doses because it's the right

poison, and I was full of poison anyway.

FLORIDA MAN ACCUSED OF USING KOOL-AID PACKETS TO STEAL NEARLY $1,000 IN WALMART MERCHANDISE, A REQUIEM

Listen here you dumb fuck taser toting khaki slacks loss prevention dipshit: felony grand theft is when the value of the stolen items exceeds one thousand dollars, and this here scooter, GPS, and 200 pack of triple A batteries amounts to no more than nine-hundred-and-ninety-four dollars, so I need you to ask yourself if this is even worth your time. For instance, I know that the average hourly wage of a Walmart loss prevention officer is $14.75 and, meaning no offense here, your jawline acne and uncreased dress shoes tell me that you don't have just a ton of seniority, so I can't imagine you're making much more than twelve. Now let me press the issue, how is it worth about sixteen bucks and moreover your safety stopping me, a man who does not have your best interest at heart, a nothing man from nowhere, from taking a non-felony amount of plastic and aluminum? The Walton family is worth two-hundred-and-thirty-five billion dollars, did you know that? Did you know that they evade paying about ten billion in taxes annually? That's enough to just straight up end homelessness in our country. That's enough cash to feed every hungry child, clean off every bird covered in damn oil, prevent every bridge from ever collapsing again, and still have some scratch left over for fireworks and vape juice. If we're talking Loss Prevention, sir, I think that the only correct way to do your job would be if you assisted me in stealing lumber, lawnmower blades, and new tires for my Kia Soul, then we drive ourselves to Arkansas to set up a motherfuckin guillotine on the lawns of some motherfuckin capitalists. If a dragon is hoarding gold is it not the duty of knights to separate the dragon from its head? Are we not knights, sir? Do we not ride into battle every time we put on a polo shirt with a logo emblazoned over the heart? It might not be a badge we chose but we shall wear it in the face of destruction. We shall stride into the unknown, arms open, because it is either that or disappear entirely— I'm sorry what was that? Felony theft in Florida is anything over $750? Got dangit.

EKPHRASIS, WITCHES' SABBATH, GOYA, 1798

First of all, dope. Who wouldn't
want to go to a party with a giant
goat? And sure, there are some
jacked up babies, but sometimes
babies are just ugly? Sometimes babies
are transparent aliens so who am I
to judge the hideous babies hanging out
at this rad goat party? Oh shit I just
noticed there are bats. Bats at a goat
party? Sick. And let's say for the sake
of argument that the goat actually is
the devil and that the babies actually
are being sacrificed, how is that not
a win for everyone? The moms don't
have to be moms anymore, which
they clearly didn't want to be, the babies
don't have to be raised by the kind
of moms who would sacrifice them
to the devil, and Satan gets to fill out
his all-baby AC/DC cover band. Bats
just get to keep doing bat stuff,
which is unassailable and always
necessary. Also the goat has a flower
crown. Ten out of ten, excellent
sabbath, next time will bring baby.

NOTES APP EXCERPT: HORMEL PEPPERONI GUY ONE MAN BAND DEPRESSION

Ok I just Googled it and apparently
the Hormel Pepperoni Guy was an ad
a few years ago in which a dude frantically,
manically? desperately plays a one-man-band
song about, you guessed it, pepperoni,
and apparently past Neil was hammered
and also identified with this processed
meat ad enough to command future me, who
has not agreed to this bullshit, to jot
down my feelings about it. So here goes:

I too am loud and obnoxious
about the wrong things. My

personality has often been compared
to an accordion in an empty

room. Stay with the accordion:
I often feel like an antique

someone hauled across an ocean
in a suitcase. I often proclaim

my existence in a way that makes
people leave. The pepperoni guy

has greasy hair, how could he not,
and teeth clenched too tight
for a song about spicy sausage. He has
clearly decided to *earn* this paycheck,
and I get it, I've done shows at noon
for no one and walked away with rent.
I have multiple times yelled

the phrase shut up you fucking drunks
I'm trying to be vulnerable up here.
That's it, I think; that's why
I feel for the pepperoni guy. I know
what it's like to do something
nobody asked for and, because
it's your job, to do it as loud
as you possibly can.

THE DIFFERENCE BETWEEN DOING AND BEING

There are two kinds of goodness in the world:
that which you plan and that which happens
by accident. Driving your girlfriend out
to the lake because it's her birthday versus
skinny dipping in that lake because she just
lost her job. It's hardest to be good when
the accidents get in the way of the stuff
you planned. You're bringing Ethiopian food
to your friend Daria, who has pneumonia,
and you see a car run into a parked car
and drive away. Here is maybe the most
controversial thing I believe: you are a good person
no matter what you do here. If you run down
the beige Ford Taurus and capture its plate
number at a stoplight, that's good. If you
watch the tan bull fade into the sunset and then
go in the side door Daria never locks, misir
wat still too hot to eat, that's good. No one ever
asked if you wanted to take part in this life.
You were just born and now you have to pay taxes
and wash your hair. I always thought I could
never truly be good unless I sprinted unthinking
into a forest or dragged a child from fire
into darkness, and how dumb is that, thinking
that my immediate reactions define who I am.
My brain thinks all kinds of shit that comes from
me but isn't all of me. I am not my thoughts. I am
a person and I have thoughts. I am a whole engine,
not just the gasoline. To be good, all you have to do
is try to be good. Even if you've got cracked windows
and no door, be someone's shelter. Throw
the ball for the dog even though you can't throw
very far. You might be wrong sometimes. You might
trip in the grocery store parking lot and drop

that dozen eggs and strawberries. You might
drive a hundred miles in the wrong direction,
but you're still on your way. You might mess up
everything you try, but you still have to,
you know. You still have to try.

SOFT SENTINEL

The best light in the house is, of course,
the one over the stove. I'm writing this

by it now. It's what doesn't wake my wife
when it's three AM for the third week

in a row. It tells me when the soup
is done. It keeps me warm

despite it being so, so small.

MERGING THE BOOK COLLECTIONS

Joint bank accounts are for Boomers, so
let the true evidence of our commitment
be this irreversible mixing. The hardest
part will actually be painting all the used
shelves you got on craigslist. The books
are just gonna go on them Dewey
Decimaled and alphabetized. No worries
about which duplicates to keep
because we don't like to read
the same stuff and here's the thing:
we don't have to have the same taste
in art in order for me to love you.
You don't have to watch horror movies
if you want to hold my hand in the dark.
I know Prince already wrote this song,
but I've got more questions and he's not
here anymore, so I guess I'll have to fling
my uncertainties into the dark: Which
truck stop actually has the best coffee
in Iowa? If a hurricane crosses
the equator does it start to build
homes? Prince, when you said hi to me
in Pizza Lucé in 2009 were you saying
hi to me or the guy at the next table?
So Anny, all the books are gonna live
together soon, and I need you to know
that no matter how many tomes
about the Bronze Age collapse
I fall asleep on, no matter how many
bootleg videos of Shoshana Bean
as Elphaba you watch on YouTube,
I will never love anyone more
than I love you right now, so come on,
let's start *The Conjuring* before
the pasta gets cold.

BOGGY CREEK MUST BE A TRIBUTARY OF THE STYX

*Author's note: The Fouke Monster, also known as the Beast of Boggy Creek,
is the Bigfoot of southwestern Arkansas. He's seven feet tall, has glowing red
eyes, and smells terrible. The author loves him.*

At the border of Whenever and Wherever, I meet
the Fouke Monster. His fingertips brush the tops
of his impossibly hairy feet and he smells, frankly,
like farts. He grunts at me to follow him
and his grunts sound, unfortunately for him
and me, like farts. We get the spirit guides
we deserve. I'm not traversing the ether fast enough
so he takes my hand in his. His hair is bristly
but his palms are smooth, like an orangutan
that's gotten a manicure. I try to ask him
what it's like to be the only one of your kind.
If it's lonely to be so lonely or if you get comfortable
with your thoughts when you have no choice but
to confront them. Only the wind answers. We get
to the precipice of nothing and look out over
nothing and nothing is below or above,
we came from something but now that's nothing
too. Your childhood home with a sign out front
proclaiming _sold_. Sidewalk chalk devoured
by a sinkhole. So here we are nowhere and it's now
and Foukey toots at me to jump. I tell him I'm scared
so he toots that with no ground to meet, falling
is just flying. I'm still hesitant so he flings me off
because growth and healing don't happen
on your fucking timetable, Neil. You can't go Nowhere
and see the Grand Nothing if you stay in the nowhere
that is your house. The house is warm and you don't
always have to be warm. The house holds you even
though you're capable of holding yourself. The house
kept you safe and it is no longer useful to be safe.
The Fouke Monster is right. It's time to find out
what's next.

THE STAKES

Because there is no way to prevent the world

from re-becoming fire, and because I'm trying
to love myself more, here is what

I'm proud of: every dog who ever wanted them

received from me Extra Pets; I drove enough
to circle the earth at least ten times

and never crashed the car; even though I gave

my love to people who might not have deserved it
I knew that love is not a finite resource; even if

I was a bad roommate I was a good friend; if

someone asked me for help, I helped them; when
presented with a fence and a brush, I painted

the whole goddamn fucking thing.

WATER IS DISTANTLY RELATED TO ALL OTHER WATER

It's early November and we're walking
around the lake. Well, I'm walking and Zoey

is running between sniffing opportunities. No one
else is at the lake despite its clear asphalt
and views of every nice house in Saint
Paul. No one else is at the lake because

I'm self-employed, which is a fancy way
of saying I take my dog for long walks

at 2 PM on a Tuesday. The paddleboat
rental shack is boarded up for the season,
the friendly swans hibernating inside. In July
the aquatic plants were so thick you almost

believed you could walk out past the shore
and feed the fish that diligently try to swallow

the sky, but now it's November and all the duckweed
has gone for the winter like parents heading south
in an RV. When I was ten I almost drowned
in the lake down the street. On the maps

it's Taylor Lake, but real ones know its real name:
Mud Lake. It must have been a prolific mud-breeding

season that year because I was wakeboarding—yes,
I know—and my board got stuck in the mud
after I biffed particularly hard. I'm talking
eight feet of air with no plan for coming down.

I'm talking Icarus clutching a ski rope. I wiped
out so hard I was briefly nuclear, and the bindings

that were supposed to keep me in the board
were, but suddenly the board was in the mud
which was under the brown, brown water.
There was this tunnel between me

and the surface, a passage between
the world of lights and breakfast and me,

small boy just trying to fly, a backward path
to heaven where the bright light is the sun
and the relatives calling to me are my dad
and brother wondering where I've gone.

I say often that I'm sure I'm not going to
kill myself, and here's how I know: when given

the choice to either stay in my watery kingdom
or return to the world where I changed
and decided nothing, I shucked off my boots
and swam. I could have been the Emperor

of Mud Lake, forever haunting its silty, stinking
shores, all I had to do was nothing. It's the easiest

thing in the world to not swim. The water is warm
enough to be confused for arms. The bubbles
swimming past could be taken for planets. Fish
are always either approaching or running

away. I don't have to be here, but I want to.
I want every day more life. Whether I'm circling

or underneath the lake, when my breath catches
and I'm drawn downward and the light begins
to fade, I cut myself free, and I swim.

WHEN I'M ALLOWED OUT OF MY HOUSE AGAIN, ASSUMING BY THEN I'VE GOT MY MEDS FIGURED OUT, IT'S OVER FOR YOU BITCHES

I'm gonna drive to Kansas City
just for lunch and a high five

from a record store employee.
My new greeting will be

a rigorous toe inspection. I'm not
into feet but I no longer

want to deny myself any
opportunities. Before this

I was certain that I did not
want to try eating durian, you

know the fruit that smells
like an armpit and tastes

like two armpits, but maybe
I like that now. Maybe I like

feeding sharks from inside
a clearly inadequate cage. Maybe

God is real and I just haven't been
to the one church where He

actually lives. Once I allow
myself out of my comfy little

end-of-days box, assuming
I've figured out the right balance

of Lexapro, Buspirone, psilocybin,
caffeine, THC, and sad but energetic

songs, it's over for you bitches.
I'm gonna stare at your toes

and then I'm gonna run this
motherfucker.

JACKETS

Today I got overwhelmed when I saw someone
wearing a jacket. Let me explain. I took my
wife to a nice patio for a nice meal because
she did something rad at work because she is
a rad person. She does many things I'm not sure I could
handle—wear bras, love me—but I really couldn't
sit in a windowless office and make small talk
with her *fucking coworkers*. Happily no one has asked me
to do any of that. Anyway she managed to get something
important done while also not killing any dolts
in polos and khakis, so we're on a patio
a little before we should be. It's warm but a cold
wind is blowing like some uncle put trick candles
on its cake. Two ladies walk up to the host stand
wearing jackets and my mind wanders—if you can
sprint while wandering—to an image of them
putting on those jackets. Jackets light enough
to layer under other jackets but heavy enough
for this day, under sixty but well above freezing, jackets
bought specifically for this purpose. You have to
not only know you need a jacket like that, but then
you have to actually go out and buy one, then you have
to keep it in your closet for most months, then you have
to deprive it of its hanger, find five dollars in the pocket, buy
yourself a coffee with those five dollars, then drive
your car without running into anything to get to
the patio at six, the time you said you'd be there,
and there are about a hundred people on this patio, so
about a hundred jackets, a hundred plans and bank
accounts and overlapping friendships; I'm imagining
putting on a hundred jackets and driving a
hundred places. I'm calling the doctor
every morning. I'm spending the whole day cleaning
the bedroom. I guess I should stop telling myself

I'm not really depressed. If someone wearing
a jacket makes me want to lay and stay
down I'm probably not just using depression
to manipulate the people I love, so here's,
I guess, to jackets. Here's to wanting to be dead
and going to work anyway. Here's to you,
my love, you made it here and I'm so happy
I get to join you.

KING OF THE GODS OF HEAVEN AND THE UNDERWORLD

To burn the wood you must first acquire the wood.
Two ways to do that: with money or an axe, and only
one of those is fun. You have to use money
to get the axe, but we won't tell anyone. To burn
the wood you must make it small enough

to burn. To make it small you have to find the tree
that's asked to be something new and bring to it
the sharp extensions of your arms. To make yourself
sharper you have to ask where the edged things
live. You have to want to be warm enough to venture

into the cold. To become warm you must first
admit, out loud, to someone who cares
about you, that you are not strong enough
to swing an eight-pound splitting maul
more than a couple times. To become warm you must

believe them when they say you will get stronger.
To get stronger you must burn offerings
to Marduk, Child of the Sun, or in the event
of the fall of Babylon, burn firewood in the chimney.
Actually, fuck Marduk, burn offerings to yourself.

Burn only that which you found in the woods with
your hands and with your hands made small
enough for the hearth. Soon you will be stronger,
you'll be who you imagined would save you as a child,
and the need for warmth will guide you there.

RALEIGH IN A SNOW GLOBE

after The Cyborg Jillian Weise

First, nothing *falls* here. I can hear you
Saying, "Neil, rain falls basically everywhere"
and you, straw man, are stupid. The rain
here goes from the clouds to the ground
skipping the space between, which is so
humid it was basically rain to begin
with—ok you're right, straw man with the voice
of my therapist, I'm talking about the weather
again. I talk about the inconsequential
in hopes that time will run out before
I have to say something I mean. Here is what
I least want to acknowledge right now:
part of me doesn't want to get better.
The gross and dumb part of me liked drinking
alone and not answering texts. It's corny,
I know, but I miss 3 AM. Since the meds
and therapy started working we don't get to
kiss each other goodnight anymore. He is
turning off the light while I'm getting up
to feed the chickens. It never snows
in Raleigh, but over the horizon comes the rain.

OPPORTUNITY, WAKE UP!

On Mars, in the middle of
a dust storm, the last words
of the Opportunity rover were
"My battery is low and it's
getting dark." Sure,
they weren't words, they were
readings, but the readings were
low battery, blocked solar panels.
For a month of Earth time
there had been a storm
and her solar panels were
shrouded in stellar debris.
Her small wings in a small
world, covered in dirt.
She wouldn't have enough power
to start back up once the sun
returned. Her: the NASA engineers
called the rover *her*, affectionately
referred to her as Oppy. Oppy,
this little robot so far from home,
was only supposed to last for two
months, and here she was fifteen
years later, finding evidence of water
and singing herself happy birthday.
She was a sparrow over blue
ocean. She was shipwrecked
on a sparse red island. Oppy,
small metal dog. Hope on six wheels.
Daydream that maybe we are not
alone. Oppy, how did you do it?
I get lonely halfway between my house
and Chicago. I feel lonesome
when the cell service drops out.
If I'm alone in a hotel room

for two days I forget how
to speak. What if over the next
ridge is nothing? What if
all this work was to get somewhere
no one is alive? Where can I stop
that someone might find me? If
a thousand years from now an object flies
overhead snapping pictures, what
is the right message to scrawl
in the dirt? What SOS will say
I was here, I was here and I tried
so hard to be here? Oppy, where
do we go when our work is done
and how will we know when it's time?
The NASA engineers, reaching
toward their still and silent friend,
played her songs through the radio.
Rocket Man. Space Oddity. I Will
Survive. The Trooper, Dust in
the Wind, Here Comes the Sun.
She couldn't hear, she never
could, she's a robot, after all,
but they still wanted their little
buddy to know how alone
she never was. Opportunity,
wake up, they said. Opportunity,
we miss you. Oppy, we love you,
we do, goodnight.

III

*Say we spend our last moments staring
at each other, hands knotted together,
clutching the dog, watching the sky burn.
Say, It doesn't matter. Say, That would be
enough. Say you'd still want this: us alive,
right here, feeling lucky.*

—Ada Limón

ABOUT EVERY 75 YEARS

Samuel Langhorne Clemens is born
November 30th, 1835. That same year, Halley's
Comet sears its way across the sky. Dirty snowball
harbinger, long-tailed master of the universe.
Of course a comet is not a baby
in Missouri. A comet does not care that a tiny
thing is learning sounds that have the potential

to become words. A comet just does comet stuff:
be unknowable, deposit plague, portend
the downfall of kings, you know. So a comet
is a comet and a boy is a boy. A boy becomes
a longer, funnier boy and names himself

after the exclamations of men at work. A boy
writes some things that I don't care about
but that people I care about care about
deeply. An ant follows trails laid out
by generations of ants before. Night precedes
day every time. Of course Mark Twain isn't born
because of the comet. He doesn't even die

because of its return. If enough people of fame
and infamy are born, one of them will die
75 years later. I know that things just happen.
Somewhere, something is always happening. Smash
dots together to form a line. Press enough lines

into one another and you get the sky. I know
I don't really matter but if I'm going to
keep doing this I have to believe I matter,
so give me a damn comet. Send something
across the night sky that points where
I should go. Let them say that my birth
predicted something other than my death.

SCIURUS VULGARIS

Once, in Paris, the only time I've ever been
to Paris, a squirrel shit on my head. I know
it was a squirrel because I saw him
in the tree right after, tiny criminal
proud of his transgressions, staring me down
as if to say, "And I'd do it again,
motherfucker." He said this in a French
accent because we were, after all,
in France. So Sarah, with whom I'd fallen
big dumb wild in love on this trip
in the way that only an American
in Italy can—see, our group went to Athens
then Rome then Florence then Paris, how
could I not have fallen in love with
someone—Sarah said she saw a bathroom
nearby and led me by the hand toward
where she thought it might have been.
She had to lead me because I was entirely
focused on wiping squirrel shit
out of my eye. Jean-Jacques the Squirrel
must have been subsisting solely on prunes
and cigarettes because this was such
a runny dump it doesn't even feel right
to call it shit. Ass gravy, maybe. Crap
cascade. So this squirrel has butt pissed
in my eye but maybe there is a god
because now the love of my life Sarah
is holding my hand. She's telling me
I'll be fine while straining to contain
a giant laugh. She is gravity: she is what
keeps everything close even as she spins.
Her palm is warm against mine but
her rings are smooth and cool. She chews
her nails so nothing but fingertips

grace the back of my hand. She's never
held my hand before this moment. Tonight
she's going to kiss me in a stairwell
overlooking the Champs-Elysées but right
now I don't know that. Right now I'm just
a boy covered in flames, fully incandescent.
We never did find that bathroom because,
and I swear this is true, I would never lie
to you, not about this, not about her, the clouds
sheared open and rain, real rain, clear, clean
rain fell all over us and we just stood there
like warm scarecrows, arms out, the water
washing away our can't sleep and won't
answer the phone, no more fear or shame,
only water: O easily breakable sky, O planes
and boats and trains that brought us
to that plaza in that city built of light, O reasons
to stay and how they are outnumbered
by reasons to go, O the going, the pushing off
into dawn even though the sun is in
our eyes, O the hands of fate and time
and Sarah and how they always know where
to find me, O let me dream of nothing
but warm radiators and a pantry
that is always full, let me never make
two wrong turns in a row, O let me
be desecrated by rodents every day
if it means that I get to go again to Paris
with the rain coming down and the summer
hurtling toward its fevered orange end
and my hand there in her impossible hand.

MY GOD, IT'S FULL OF STARS

I want to be
One notch below bedlam, like a radio without a dial.
—Tracy K. Smith

1.

It's not that I want to be obnoxious—
if it takes ten thousand hours
to become an expert at something
then I just *am* obnoxious. It's more
that I want to be undeniable. When
I enter a room I want you to know
I am there even if I am not
speaking. I want to be what turns
humans into moths. The thing moths
need to know is that the moon
was never within their grasp.
Moths need to know it is better
to have a fake moon right here
than a real one far away.

2.

You can put your hand through anything
if you either don't care about your hand
or if you recognize that your hand is atoms
and the thing is atoms. If the atoms would
cooperate and let each other past, then what
would be the point of a door? It's the difference
between looking and seeing; you could put
your hand through a window or
you could put your hand *through* it.

3.

I'm searching my pockets for crucifixes. I'm praying
in languages I don't understand. I'm painting
pentagrams on trees and never returning
to them. Some kid might be scared on the walk

to school by the faded star in a circle, but I'll
never know. We almost never get to
see the extent of the good or ill we do.
After you cast a spell you have to forget
you cast it. The mere act of observing
something changes its behavior. Ask
quarks and the citizens of London. You plant
a garden and then it's the garden's problem.

4.

Everything does happen for a reason, but most
often that reason is stupid. Neglected power lines
at the center of a forest fire. A heart attack
during a horror movie. Hanlon's Razor applies
to the universe too: things happen merely
because other things happened before.

5.

If, released from purpose, I get to decide
my own, here is what I'd like to be: a concrete floor,
cured and newly painted. A shade tree among
plenty of shade trees. The night that follows
the day every time. I want to be unobtrusive,
and useful, and there.

PRAYER TO THE MINOR DEITY OF LEFT TURNS

Let the light just be green today. A week

of reds after this, but today I just cannot

sit still. Today I need to drag something

across something, so let the light be green.

Let the traffic clear when it's about to be

my turn. I have been making sure these wheels

stay in line and now I want to wrench them

diagonal. Let the lights come on when they are

supposed to, the street- head- and tail-lights,

the flashlights and stars, the green arrow,

let them all arrive exactly when they are ordained.

AUGUST 8TH, 1969, IAIN MACMILLAN TAKES HIS
PHOTOGRAPH OF THE BEATLES CROSSING THE STREET

First, 69, nice. Second, it's not that
I don't like The Beatles, it's that
I don't learn anything from them.
Maybe if it was the 60s and I couldn't
hear a sitar whenever I wanted
just by asking my doom rectangle,
but even when I started listening
to music in 2001 (you know how
you hear music before that
but it was never something you chose)
I was sort of unimpressed, but,
having said all that, third, Octopus's
Garden is a fuckin slapper. Octopus's Garden
could spit in my hand and steal
my wallet and I'd still ask it
on a second date. Like literally
Ringo was hanging out on Peter
Sellers's yacht in around or near
Greece and someone told him, passing
the blunt like an Olympic torch, that
octopuses make gardens from troves
of shiny bullshit, and Ringo, knowing
he gets only one song per album, said,
"Alright lads, this one's about a mollusc!"
What poise and grace from the least
talented Beatle. What a power move
to look at people trying to make A Statement
and respond, "No, this is what I have
to say. Stuff up here is hard. I'd prefer
to be under all this, in the shade,
with some shiny junk
and an octopus."

I HOPE YOU DANCE (UNTIL YOU ARE DEAD)

With apologies to and repudiation of Lee Ann Womack

I hope you win a lifetime supply of Chili's fajitas just before Chili's leaves your town. You can keep the supply, but now the closest Chili's is three hours away. In other words, I hope your dreams coming true turns out to be a massive inconvenience. I hope the day you discover you are afraid of whales is the day your boyfriend proposes to you while swimming with them. I wish you a thousand balloons and no fucking helium. I hope every Grand Canyon is secluded in fog, every world heritage site dripping in scaffolding, every scenic route beginning and ending next to a highway porn shop. I hope you only get Tinder matches on your last day of vacation. I hope you inherit your dream house but it's in New Jersey which is the state with the highest property tax rate and also the state that is New Jersey. I hope all your plane tickets are twenty dollars and standby. I hope you look at a mountain and can only think "Cool, a mountain." I hope you get paid regular, first of the month, but it has to come by mail, as a check, and I hope your mailbox is full of ants. And when you get the choice to sit it out or dance, I hope you dance, but it's one of those Medieval dancing plagues so yeah, fucker, I hope you dance. Let's all boogie until we're dead. May Saint Vitus's dance carry us to hell.

WALTZ FOR A DOOMED RELATIONSHIP

There are a lot of fun things you can do
with your roommate, and having sex
with them is one thing you're never,
ever allowed to do. So the night we signed

the lease I was having sex with my roommate
and she asked if I wanted to go with her
to help out on her ex-boyfriend's parents'
farm. "Sure," I said, stupidly, but I was 22,

had never made a good decision, and saw
no need to start then. It was night in Stockholm,
Wisconsin, where the fireflies outnumber
the stars. She was sitting on the trunk

of her car, giant blue sedan, ship of the Midwest
fields. I was facing her with both hands on her thighs.
She was cradling the base of my skull and lifting
me slightly toward her because I wasn't quite

tall enough to kiss her without straining. Blame
it on the locked knees or the seven beers
or the making out aggressively after digging
a garden in the sun, blame it on whatever

wrongheaded idea you want, but I passed out
into the grass. I was a pile of elbows
and eyelashes there under the stars. And under
the stars she asked me if I wanted her to

join me there on the grass under the stars,
and I said I needed water but she must have heard
yes so she lay in the crook my elbow accidentally
made, put her head on my chest, and there

under the stars we must have slept
because the next thing I remember is the mist
rising off the fields, the bugs rising from
the mist, the sun behind it all, that bastard the sun.

THE NATURE OF NAILS

Nails rust because it's in the nature
of nails. A casket, no matter how
well-intentioned, is just a box,
and all boxes one day lose too many
sides to contain anything. Dirt seems
like it's all part of one thing, the earth,
until a shovel grabs it, which is when
it becomes dirt. A tree grows into
the dirt after it's become earth again,
and let's say the tree is deciduous
so every year the leaves leave
and return, everything on this spot
flies apart but eventually comes back
together. The leaves that leave become
dirt (at least if you leave them alone).
Put whatever you need in the box,
knowing that nothing is contained
forever. I drop in my first car
accident and the times I could have
helped and didn't. The stolen answers
from that one Bio exam. The gunshot
and the blood I could only run away
from. The head injuries that were
my fault. The gear stripped of its teeth
for no reason, my hands that made
all these mistakes. I made the shovel
relinquish its dirt. I am alone
on this hill, just the box, the shovel,
the earth, the ghost of the tree, and me.

THE TIME A KID PULLED A KNIFE ON ME SO I PULLED A KNIFE ON HIM

It's August I think? I'm wearing shorts
and the breeze doesn't cool off anything
so it's probably August. Anny is taking
the train home late from a work event
and I drive to meet her because yesterday someone
followed her shouting for three blocks
and the day before that there were gunshots
as soon as the train flopped open
its doors. I park in the back of the Target
parking lot, the part near University
that never gets used. The back
of every Target parking lot is lonely
like Kansas. She texts to say she is
three stops away from Hamline, so I wander
to the platform. Just as I lean against
a mercifully cold steel pillar three kids
roll up to me. The kid in back is wearing
a blue hoodie and carrying a stack
of pizza boxes. The kid in the middle
I don't remember anything about
because the kid in front says he likes
my shirt, asks what band it is, and before
I can answer flicks open his knife
and asks if I like it. I'm not a smooth
person without rehearsal but I don't
hesitate before I snap open
my bigger, shinier knife and tell him
I like mine more. The kids are all twelve,
thirteen maybe, and there we are, alone
on a train platform in Saint Paul
in August, alone as you can be
under surveillance, alone, pointed
at each other. His knife is bright,
metallic, all luminous red, half-

serrated, seven dollars at a gas station.
Mine is matte grey steel with a curved
point, designed to slide between
skin and muscle, about a hundred
bucks from a Cabela's in South
Dakota because I just couldn't
drive anymore. We float in circles,
just us, the night, and the knives. I close
mine and two seconds later, a second
after I'd have liked, he closes his.
Anny's train arrives and the doors
slouch open like the exhausted tools
they are. The kids pile on, shouting,
Bye dude! over their shoulders. Anny
and I walk to the car and she asks me
how my day was. I say, shaking less
than now I think I should have been,
"I think I was just almost mugged? I don't
know." The night ends whenever it decides.

I PUT ON MY SOCKS IN THE WRONG ORDER AND NOW I'M GONNA GET HIT BY A CAR

I think as I put on my boots anyway. I'm supposed to
resist compulsions when I feel capable

because it makes the misfiring neurons weaker, and today

I'm feeling capable of lots of stuff, so I guess that means
today I'm fighting my brain. When the brain says,
"You're gonna bleed out on the sidewalk,"

I'll say, "Then the grass will have something

to drink." When the brain says, "This is the day

you go to the bridge," I'll say, "But there are

so many bridges." Nothing gets to want me
dead and avoid the consequences. You'll get
the socks you get, brain, we're going to the airport.

THE EARL OF

Putting aside, for a moment, people,
the thing at the top of the list of what
I'd die for is sandwiches. People have
been, on balance, a terrible idea,
but sandwiches never make you feel
wrong unless you make them wrong. Two walls
of bread and whatever they can contain.
The boundaries of the universe, if we are
letting mayo, pickles, and whatever else
represent whatever else is out there.
Give me a long enough sandwich
and a place to stand and I will move
the earth. If I have seen further it is
by standing on the sandwiches
of giants. Once I was driving through
Cleveland at half past bastard
when there came The Sign: Melt
Bar and Grilled. A grilled cheese
with kimchi on it and I could then
finish slow sailing all the way
to Toronto. Toronto and Buffalo are
the bread around Lake Ontario. The US
and Canada are the bagel halves
and I am the cream cheese.
A poem is a sandwich in which
something messy is neatly contained.
I take a pill in the morning and a pill
at night and my day becomes
a sandwich. I am the bread
and you are the bread and we
hold love between us. If forced
by some unfair devil to choose: death
or continue on in a world without
sandwiches, I'd live, I'd choose to live

because I have every day so far and I can't
imagine stopping soon but at night,
in bed, the blanket and mattress my whole
wheat armor, I'd dream of that which
is held first outside then inside. I'd dream
of all that could be, just waiting to be built.

DELUGE

The quietest moment ever, at least
for me, at least that I can remember,
was about a year ago when I woke
up at 4:48 AM covered in sweat.
4 AM is, unfortunately, the most
poetic time, which also makes it
the corniest. Peace is corny, as are
joy, contentment, and a sense
of belonging. It's actually pretty
frustrating that the only cool
emotions are yearning and a concern
for others. It's actually really
frustrating because of how much
time I've spent trying to be cool
when I could have just had
a strong desire for someone
far away from me to be happy.
It's 4:48 AM and I've just woken
up drenched. It sounds like
a late August storm might be
striding in so I go out on the back
porch to confirm my suspicions.
The porch is just a glorified
fire escape because I live in a condo
in a city, the same city I've lived in
since the one that raised me,
and here in Saint Paul we don't
get more than we deserve.
Minneapolis is the first
of the Western cities and Saint Paul
is the last of the East. We're at
the tail end of the Midwest
at the tail end of this last age.
The Holocene is almost over

and we're just waiting for the lake
to freeze enough to hold us
and our skates. I go out
to the barely a porch
and I let the wind fold
over me. I lean out over the cold
railing and the painted boards
flake off under my feet. There's
thunder and there's lightning
in the distance but they don't have
anything to do with me
yet. I'd trade most of my other,
lesser moments for this
moment. This moment stretches
out like a newly-adopted cat
discovering a sunbeam. This
moment requires no encouragement
to sing. This moment ends,
of course, but even now
it holds my hand
as it beckons me to sleep.

A THIRD PLACE

Here's a picture: a cloud of dust
rising over the dog park as the sun
transits toward the horizon. Yes I am
talking about the dog park again. I don't
go anywhere else. Or, I do, but I don't
like being there: the grocery store
or the soccer stadium, the midnight
street outside my house, they all
give me hives, usually not literally
though sometimes literally, usually
just like I am full of bees and the bees
are trying to warn me of something.
You know the Romans told the future
by watching bees. A swarm at dawn
meant time to gather stones. The hive
completely still for exactly one hour
meant the coming death
of the emperor, so if we agree
that bees are prophets and if
we agree that there are in fact
bees inside me not just incorrect
chemicals, then perhaps the bees
are making a prediction. Rifles
at the soccer game, disease hiding
amongst the avocadoes, and that
it hasn't happened yet doesn't mean
the bees are wrong, bees just have
a longer view of things. So that's why
it seems like I only go to the dog park.
At the dog park no one stands too close
to anyone; Zoey is there to sniff and run,
sure, but her main interest is protecting
me; no one there can ask me to sign
a petition or answer my phone; at

the dog park it's always four PM and the sun
is always thrusting its arms through
the dust clouds thrown up by dogs
just being dogs and somewhere
among the haze and tall grass,
somewhere in there is me.

OUR NUMBERED DAYS

Have you ever been in love? Horrible, isn't it? It makes you so
vulnerable.
　　　　—Neil Gaiman

You are always ticking inside of me.
　　　　—Sierra DeMulder

The one you love and the one who loves you are never, ever the same
person.
　　　　—Chuck Palahniuk

Maybe one body is simply insufficient.
　　　　—Catie Rosemurgy

I leave the door unlocked, I leave the lights on.
　　　　—The author

If I can stop one heart from breaking, I shall not live in vain.
　　　　—Emily Dickinson

Any fool can be happy.
　　　　—Clive Barker

They say when you are missing someone that they are probably
feeling the same, but I don't think it's possible for you to miss me as
much as I'm missing you right now
　　　　—Edna St. Vincent Millay

I used to think that love was two people
driving through police barricades

while shotgunning Red Bull, or maybe
it was pushing the boat away from shore

regardless of the wind. You said love meant
the mutual keeping of secrets, like number

of alleys vomited in, like kisses behind
ears, so I became a puzzle box. I stored

the details of you inside me and decided
that keeping quiet kept you mine.

All that's over now, so here is what
I remember: you like hazelnut

in your coffee; you're a better driver
when the car has a stick shift

because that means you can't
text and drive; you have a scar

on your left shoulder from the time
you were so plastered in a December

Minnesota gay bar that you didn't
notice you were leaning on a

radiator; once your faucet was dripping
and it took you two months to call

the landlord; you forget to drink
the tea and then complain when it is

cold; you're late to the airport but early
to funerals; you ask for what you are

unwilling to give; you overstay
your every welcome; your favorite color

is Bakelite seafoam green; you loved me
once. Though it wasn't for very long,

though it was distracted, though
you reminded everyone that it shouldn't

have happened, I was there,
I saw it, you loved me.

A TIRADE AGAINST HOT TUBS GIVING WAY TO THE UNIVERSAL CONSCIOUSNESS

It's not just that I have OCD. I do, very
bad—I wash my hands until they bleed
and my brain has made me think about
killing myself every half-hour since
I was fourteen—but I refuse to have
my hatred of hot tubs essentialized
to just my mental illness. I hate
hot tubs because they are biology
experiments you are supposed to
relax in. What do bacteria like? Warm.
Wet. What are hot tubs?
                                        A hot tub
is a slow cooker for staph infections.
Hot tubs are what you would get
if pink eye had advertising. I hate hot
tubs more than my dad because at least
my dad never pretended this was all supposed to
be fun. Ok so let's also not essentialize OCD
to just germs; I am worried about
so much more than germs. Humans
are just rocks that got squishy and learned
how to think, right? Most of everything
everywhere is oxygen, hydrogen, nitrogen,
and carbon. People are just peculiar
concentrations of those four things,
and I know it doesn't make sense to think
like this, but if those things flake off
of someone they are imbued with that
someone's energy, and I, a separate
someone with my own discrete socks
and calendars, stones thrown and stones
kept in the hand, things to do, things
to never do again, might touch their

molecules, and what's to stop me becoming
a little more them? If we're all just atoms
that like different music what's to stop me
from shaking hands and suddenly caring
about jazz? Hot tubs accelerate
the process, they make of all of us
one soup. From soup we formed and to soup
we shall return. Soup is warm and helps you
to live. Once everything was soup and then
in that soup something moved. The only
difference between me and an exploding
star is that I am afraid to fall apart. The only
thing that makes you not me is where
we woke up today. We're just a couple flakes
of stars and the time it takes to get
between them. Everywhere is either warm
or cold, and I didn't ask for this warmth,
but now that it's here? I'll hold it like all
the other candles have gone out.

ED WHITE ELEMENTARY, SEABROOK, TEXAS, SUMMER

It's Two-Thousand and Two,
I'm thirteen and alive,
and I just landed a ten-stair
gap on my rollerblades. Yes,
I know, rollerblades;
skateboarding is hard. Jeff
and I are out behind the
elementary school where
there lives the sketchiest
staircase in Harris
County. Cracked concrete
poorly patched with tar
at the top, pitted asphalt
strewn with gravel
at the bottom. I'm skating
harder than I need to
because if I'm gonna get hurt
I should get really
hurt. I think a 540
is the one where you land
backward, or at least I landed
backward facing the stairs.
I absolutely stomped it. First
try. Thirteen-years-old
out there dropping hammers
in my new Solomons. I'm
gonna be the next whoever
is a famous rollerblader. I am
gonna have a future
containing tens of
dollars. I spin back around
and there's Jeff, skating
toward me, no rips in his

jeans, not yet anyway, he
wants a high five, his arms
are full of flowers.

DISCARNATE

It would be too easy to say, "but home
is nowhere." I'll never see again the house
I grew up in. Not because someone took it
or took it away, I could take Lexington
to 94, 94 to 35E, 35E to 35, 35 to 45
in Dallas, 45 to NASA Road 1, NASA
1 to Lakeshore Boulevard. I could do
all that, but why? Even if I got a plane
involved, why make any effort at all
to stand outside a stack of bricks
where a bunch of trauma happened?
Joy too, I guess, but joy ends
while the bad stuff that happens to you
continues happening. You can stop it
but then you have to stop it, you know?
It'd be too easy to say home is nowhere
because then I couldn't point to where
I burned the sheets in which the bad thing
happened. No garage with the gasoline
fumes and the chirping summer heat.
How is it that a brick can leave a scar
on me and come away with no evidence
of its own? What kind of world
do we live in where a tree you love
can fall and crush not even a fence?
If I had a choice, and I do, I'd never
go back to that town again. Not to swim
in the bay or reminisce, not to
lay a single flower on a single fucking grave.

EKPHRASIS, NIGHTHAWKS, EDWARD HOPPER, 1942

I have to be honest, I don't get this
painting. Like I get that it's supposed to
represent loneliness and isolation in a city,
that the lack of details mean it could be
anywhere, that all four people are so close
to each other but separated by silence, I get
all that, but ask yourself: what city
large enough to have an all-night diner
has streets that are perfectly clean? Even
in the 40s, not one broken window? Cigarettes
back then made you fuck better and no one
is smoking? Not a single butt to be seen?
Maybe I'm just mad because a quiet place
to waste my time is one more thing denied
to me as a millennial, but damnit, Edward,
if you're gonna call someone a nighthawk,
try to give them some dirt under the nails.

HAIL THE FIRE AND THE WALL IT COULDN'T BRING DOWN

On the river bluffs overlooking Saint Paul
stands the old Hamm's brewery. The brewhouse
sent out barrels of beer in horse carts because
A it was 1890 and B there were lots of strong,
shirtless, thirsty men down at that river,
crushing tree trunks between their
thighs I think. Sorry, the unknown
makes me horny. Anyway, Hamm's was
the regional terrible beer of the upper
Midwest before Anheuser-Busch and Miller-
Coors bought out all the bad regional beers
and put *their* pissvasser in the same cans.
Anheuser-Busch is owned by AbInBev, which is
run by a bunch of Belgians, and what the
fuck do they know about terrible beer,
but I digress. By the 60s, the edifice
that had gotten so many sweaty river people
drunk was completely abandoned except
for a colony of raccoons. The tiny-handed
thieves must have been shocked that their god
was punishing them when streaks of lightning
hit the wooden-roofed barrel house. The God
of Raccoons is just a dumpster with hands. No one
is in that part of Saint Paul at night, so by the time
anyone called the red trucks the blaze
was in firm control. The fire took the roof,
windows, floor, joists, just stone stacked
on stone and the mortar that decided
not to crumble because things were just getting
interesting. All of this had to happen
so that, in the year of our lord 2021, some art
nerds could get together with some beer nerds,
buy the place, and jam it gills tits chock full
of furniture from the free section

of Craigslist, some of which I'm sitting on
right now, an hour before sunset, pretty
solid beer resting on my knee, Zoey's snoot
resting on the other, a slight breeze asking
to join us under this Minnesota sky. Sure
the sky is the same blue everywhere but here,
right now, it just seems sky blue. Blue
like the second stage of a bruise. Blue but
more so. The burnt wall is shored up
with metal posts but they're rusted,
and what is rust but slow combustion, so if
I'm going to die, let it be from the collapse
of this wall. Not now, let it be after
my dog or anyone else who loves me
has gone, but if I'm the last, let me be
the last victim of this fire.

WHAT I'VE LEARNED ABOUT ENGINES

after Gretchen Marquette

(I)

Once, the word engine meant any
piece of machinery. Latin ingenium
meaning ability. Latin motor, meaning
to move. To begin stationary and end
stationary, but for a while, to fly.

(II)

Because I don't really have a dad, these facts
are going to be from Wikipedia. More like
Wiki*pa*dia, am I right.

(III)

Rudolf Diesel is why it's called
a diesel engine. Every day we are
surrounded by ghosts and we cannot
hear them shouting their names.

(IV)

Guns are a type of internal combustion
engine. My father would be pleased
to learn this, if he'd ever call. I might
see him before his funeral, but there are so many
ways to not fix that which is broken.

(V)

Latin ingenium, like genius, like
inspiration. Like sudden certainty.
Like now I know why I had to
go through all of this, because
on the other side was here.

(VI)

And isn't it just like me to romanticize
what is trying to kill me. Ain't it so me
to depend on something to save me now
knowing it will send me to hell later.

(VII)

Motor meaning to shift. Meaning you can
get out of bed today. Meaning if you don't
like the weather you can find new clouds.
Meaning nothing must remain the same.

DICK SHARK

So let me tell you about Dick Shark.
My friend Mark was a tattoo artist, and for
Shark Week he drew a shark with a penis
for a head. He's always told me that if I ever
decide to get Dick Shark he'd put it on me
for free. Now, a cheap tattoo ain't good
and a good tattoo ain't cheap, but a free
tattoo is how you tell people you know
where to find good sandwiches and bad
drugs. So I'm contemplating
getting Dick Sharked, and I'm thinking about
all my terrible tattoos. The Metalcore album
title I got when I was eighteen. The crawfish
on my ankle. The semicolon I got,
long before it meant people had lived
through something, just because I liked
semicolons. It's a very useful punctuation
mark; shut up. The worst tattoo is the one
you get because you think someone else
will like it. If the point were to be more
likeable everyone would just get Gandhi's
face tattooed over their face. All the bad
decisions I've ever made have led me
to some form of happiness. My first
girlfriend taught me that I don't like it
when people are bad people. Being
a fencer taught me how to live
without any friends. So a needle
could make me the first and perhaps
only Dick Shark Bearer, and it occurs to me
just how soon I'll be dead. I'm someone's great
times a whole bunch grandson, and I'm amazed
I lived past 21 anyway, so why wouldn't I take
my body, my body at which I have squinted

in the mirror, my body I spend all my time
hating, why wouldn't I take that dumb lump
and make it make me laugh? Knowing you
will die is far more serious than actually
dying. I'm not often someone I can love,
so I'm going to be someone
that makes me happy. I am not yet the Sea
of the Dick Shark, but I know he's out there,
waiting, hungry for my flesh. He loves me,
as only a shark with a penis for a face
can love a man, and he can wait as long
as he needs for me to love me too.

(I AM LARGE, I CONTAIN MULTITUDES)

I would like, this evening, to make a compact
with the stars. I would like us to agree that we will
continue to glow even after we are dead. I'm not
ignoring the dirt, the dirt will come later, I just want to
begin among the stars. I would like to thank this world
that allows me to be in it even though of it I am
so very scared. I would like to thank the one therapist
in North Carolina who takes my insurance. I would
like to suggest, if your feet are cold, consider
your laptop charger. I would like to acknowledge dogs
and their willingness to receive pets from me.
I'd like to say that yours is the only permission
you need to love yourself. I'd like apples to be sweeter
and mangoes to be closer to me. I'd like eight full hours
of sleep, but I'll take five and a nap on a plane.
I'd like to hurl wishes into the fog. I would like
to be ungovernable as a possum in a darkening field.
I want to drive around the block
because the song isn't over yet. I would
prefer if the no crazy pills didn't also raise my blood
pressure. I'd like a time machine just so I can find out
if dinosaurs had feathers. I'd like to thank concrete,
snow days, the dark that's always rising. I'd like
to thank the dirt. You thought I forgot
about the dirt. The dirt holds my grandmother
and some day it will hold me. Thank you, dirt,
for doing everything with persistence
and grace. Thank you, dirt, for the mirror you hold
up to me. Thank you, stars, for making the dirt
and me, I promise to be the dirt one day.
I would like, this evening, in front of everything
that lives between here and the end, I would like to
make a promise: whatever I've got left in me,
you can have it. I've been gathering all these stones.
I think it's time to roll them all away.

HEN SONNET, OR, GOOD MORNING LADIES

I know I am letting owning chickens
become my whole deal, but I don't get to
choose the way wonderment arrives to me.
Yesterday MayBelle, once the tiniest
of the four hens, shy MayBelle who wouldn't
dare receive from you a bit of berry, scared
MayBelle, all flapping of wings and clatter
of talons on the tile, MayBelle was the first
of my first chickens to lay an egg. She'd been
yelling all day in case someone nearby
didn't know she was accomplishing something.
An ode to May, smallest parade. Ode to May,
round harbinger of the morning. Hail May-
Belle, without whom there would be no breakfast.

ASTROS @ CUBS, JUNE 10TH, NIGHT GAME

In my favorite memory it's 1998
and we're visiting family in Chicago.
In everyone's favorite memory it is always
the late 90s. Cousin Zach has just handed out
the baseball bats. No diamond can contain
us so we'll settle for this half acre. The crabapple
tree has just shed its midsummer bounty,
and Zach underhands one right to me. While
the overripe fruit is suspended in the evening,
let me say this: even if I had the chance I wouldn't
be anyone else. Sure I don't love myself,
but I've come too far to start over now.
The crabapple is waltzing toward me
and I've got so much time before it gets
here. I could do my homework and clean
up after dinner. I'm gonna grow up before I get
a chance to hit this thing. But when it does
arrive, too soon, like summer, I demolish
it. Absolute ripper. Totally cranked. The too
ripe fruit just fucking explodes. I swear
it's like a movie: we stare at each other
for a moment and then start cheering. Zach
wipes pulp from his glasses. It's 1998
and I'm from Houston so I holler "Jeff
Bagwell!" We're two boys unaware
of the precipice before us. We're just running
the bases, lawn chair, tomato cage, shed
corner, stomp home. I need you to believe me
when I say this: the second the last crabapple
has cleared the fence, the fireflies begin
their dance to call in the night. I've never seen
a firefly before. I call it a lightning bug
and Zach asks what that is. Nowhere to go

but Chicago. No time like seven minutes
after sunset. Who could be me better?
Why be anything at all?

DECEMBER 21ST, 2022, THE SOLSTICE

Here let us define the border between now
and after. Not because it exists but because it helps

the dumb lump I call my brain. I am built
to recognize patterns. I am made to place boundaries

where once there were none, and it is now my job
to fit the square peg of non-linear time into my mind's

round hole. Yes I said round hole, stop giggling,
me. Here at the goddamn border of all goddamn things

sometimes we're gonna have to sound a little silly
to get our point across. We're going to have to embarrass

ourselves in the pursuit of being Not
Alone. So, in the interest of connection to the great

unknown, here is the most humiliating thing
I am willing to admit: I am not always a good driver.

True vulnerability is hard. Give me a
minute. I'm becoming my father and I don't always hate

it. I don't know the answers
to every Jeopardy! question. If asked to change

a tire there's only a fifty-percent chance
I will do it correctly. I guess what I'm trying to say

is that I'm scared of being a liar
because I'm scared of becoming my dad. So here, at the edge

of all things, at the very precipice of now,
I release myself from the need to be right all the damn time.

I allow future me to make mistakes and know
he will still be welcomed home. I forgive myself for being

scared and causing all the pain
a scared person does. I declare here, in this long night

in the middle of this dark age, here
where the walls are thin, where through the shadow

one can see the dawn, here I say
goodbye, me, I love you. Here I leave myself and know

I will come back around.

LINER NOTES

No Part: "Crazy Love" is a Paul Simon song I think about a lot, and the name carved into the food in the fridge is lifted from my own poem "Future Tense."

Combination 1432: I checked, he's changed the combination since, so don't get any funny ideas.

Security Check: several lines from this poem are lifted directly from Scientology's question list for their "security checks," in which they interrogate their own members about ways in which they might have sinned against the cult. Yeah, I said cult. Come get me, Miscavige.

Cryoseism: a cryoseism is a fancy word for an ice quake, and The Bloop is a funny sound slash maybe Cthulu.

Turducken: Part Manimal is the name of a band my dudes Mark and Eli were in. Shout out Mark and Eli. The Smashing Pumpkins song is "Luna."

Not Avoidant Just Tired: "New vines at night" is lifted from a terrible poem by the BTK Killer. Fuck you, Dennis.

Sevens Over Kings: Shout out Doctor Zasio. I watched a lot of *Hoarders* as exposure therapy for contamination obsessions, and I genuinely think it's helped me be more ok with all the gross stuff I have to do now as a hobby farmer.

Sean: The Hatebreed song was "I Will Be Heard" and the Comeback Kid shirt was the cool one with the Turn It Around album art.

Coroner's Voice Note: Jenny is a sort of timeless character across the Mountain Goats' discography, and here I've decided she's a coroner in the 30th century.

New Chemical: This poem is an interpolation of "New Chemical Hades" by my friends Caracara.

Florida Man: This poem came from a prompt in which one googles "Florida Man [your birthday]" and then writes a persona poem from the perspective of your particular Florida Man. You're welcome.

Pepperoni Guy: That's literally all my notes app said: Hormel Pepperoni Guy One Man Band Depression

Doing and Being: "From a fire into darkness" is an image from Michael Mlekoday's poem "Sidewalk Chalk" that I think about at least once a week.

Merging the Book Collections: You know which Prince song I'm talking about. Also, Prince really did say hi to me in the Pizza Lucé on Selby Avenue in 2009. That's not a note but I had to brag about it somewhere.

Boggy Creek: "We are nowhere and it's now" is, of course, the title of a Bright Eyes song that if I don't reference once a book I'll burst into flames.

All Other Water: "The world of lights and breakfast" is also from my poem "Future Tense," from which I apparently love to repurpose lines. For a long time I was embarrassed of that poem and its melodrama, so maybe I'm revisiting these lines as a way of forgiving past Neil for his sadness over a relationship that was clearly terrible for him. "I choose more life" is an interpolation of Tony Kushner's line "I want more life" from *Angels in America.*

Opportunity, Wake Up!: The playlist is real, look it up if you wanna weep to an Iron Maiden song.

About Every 75 Years: "Somewhere, something is always happening" is an interpolation of a line from Springsteen's "Dancing in the Dark."

My God, It's Full of Stars: The poem itself is after Tracy K. Smith's poem of the same title. "The difference between looking and seeing" is part of a song title by Ceremony, "Dead Moon California (Midnight In Solitude)/The Difference Between Looking and Seeing." Everything happening for a reason but that reason being stupid is a concept I lifted from my poem "Ballad of the Bruised Lung."

The Nature of Nails: "The leaves that leave become dirt (at least if you leave them alone)." is lifted directly from the notes my editor, Michael Mlekoday, sent me on a draft of this book. I might not be a smart man, but I have learned to recognize moments of brilliance.

Deluge: the idea that Saint Paul is the last of the Eastern cities and Minneapolis is the first of the Western cities is one that Mark says all the time, and I have no idea where he got it, but I've incorporated it into my self-concept. "It's Thunder and It's Lightning" is the title of a song by We Were Promised Jetpacks.

Ed White Elementary: "Thirteen and alive" is from Anis Mojgani's poem "Here Am I." Anis Mojgani, poet laureate of both Oregon and my heart.

Discarnate: "...but home is nowhere" is the title of an AFI song, and "discarnate" is a word that features prominently in the chorus. "The sheets in which the bad thing happened" is from my poem "Moving Day."

Dick Shark: Honesty and Heresy

(I am large, I contain multitudes): the title is, of course, from Whitman's "Song of Myself, 51." "Eight Full Hours of Sleep" is the title of a song by Against Me! *The Dark Is Rising* is a children's novel by Susan Cooper that absolutely freaked me out as a kid. The possum line is inspired by the Mountain Goats song "Possum by Night."

ABOUT THE AUTHOR

Neil Hilborn is a best-selling author and, with over 150 million views to his credit, he is the most-watched poet ever. He has performed in 41 states and 8 countries, and in 2019 alone he drove coast to coast five times while on tour. His favorite touring moments are: crying while meeting a wombat in Australia; spending two weeks in Edinburgh at the Fringe Festival; meeting Dionne Warwick at the Smithsonian; and putting 12,000 miles on a minivan in two months with his fellow road goblin Mark. His favorite sandwiches come from: Primanti Bros in Pittsburgh, Black's BBQ in Austin, one specific Publix in Tampa, and a torta truck he found while stranded in Pasco, Washington. One time on stage he accidentally punched the microphone and broke his wedding ring, and thanks to years of therapy he did not interpret this as a sign. His preferred stage entrance music is "Born to Run" by Bruce Springsteen, during which he walks very slowly. In addition to touring and writing he runs workshops on craft, performance, and how to apologize for ignoring texts. He and his wife live on a hobby farm outside Chapel Hill, North Carolina, where they adopt too many animals.

AUTHOR BOOK RECOMMENDATIONS

How to Maintain Eye Contact by Robert Wood Lynn

Sometimes you get so lonely that the solitude itself reaches out of you to hold someone's hand. This book doesn't need you to stick around, but it hopes you do. I've never felt more personally assaulted than by the line "I stood by myself so long the silence got loud."

Nothing Is Okay by Rachel Wiley

Listen I know you know that this book goes hard, so let me say this: anger can itself be vulnerable. Tenderness can be a sharp edge.

I'll Fly Away by Rudy Francisco

When we were on tour in the UK, Rudy asked every employee at a hotel front desk if he could have an ironing board delivered to his room. I never saw Rudy on stage without a perfect crease. That's why you should get Rudy's book: you know he'll take care of you.

OTHER BOOKS BY BUTTON POETRY

If you enjoyed this book, please consider checking out some of our others, below. Readers like you allow us to keep broadcasting and publishing. Thank you!

Jared Singer, *Forgive Yourself These Tiny Acts of Self-Destruction*
Adam Falkner, *The Willies*
George Abraham, *Birthright*
Omar Holmon, *We Were All Someone Else Yesterday*
Rachel Wiley, *Fat Girl Finishing School*
Bianca Phipps, *crown noble*
Natasha T. Miller, *Butcher*
Kevin Kantor, *Please Come Off-Book*
Ollie Schminkey, *Dead Dad Jokes*
Reagan Myers, *Afterwards*
L.E. Bowman, *What I Learned From the Trees*
Patrick Roche, *A Socially Acceptable Breakdown*
Rachel Wiley, *Revenge Body*
Ebony Stewart, *BloodFresh*
Ebony Stewart, *Home.Girl.Hood.*
Kyle Tran Myhre, *Not A Lot of Reasons to Sing, but Enough*
Steven Willis, *A Peculiar People*
Topaz Winters, *So, Stranger*
Darius Simpson, *Never Catch Me*
Blythe Baird, *Sweet, Young, & Worried*
Siaara Freeman, *Urbanshee*
Robert Wood Lynn, *How to Maintain Eye Contact*
Junious 'Jay' Ward, *Composition*
Usman Hameedi, *Staying Right Here*
Sean Patrick Mulroy, *Hated for the Gods*
Sierra DeMulder, *Ephemera*
Taylor Mali, *Poetry By Chance*
Matt Coonan, *Toy Gun*
Matt Mason, *Rock Stars*
Miya Coleman, *Cottonmouth*
Ty Chapman, *Tartarus*
Lara Coley, *ex traction*
DeShara Suggs-Joe, *If My Flowers Bloom*
Ollie Schminkey, *Where I Dry the Flowers*
Edythe Rodriguez, *We, the Spirits*
Topaz Winters, *Portrait of My Body as a Crime I'm Still Commiting*
Zach Goldberg, *I'd Rather Be Destroyed*
Eric Sirota, *The Rent Eats First*

Available at buttonpoetry.com/shop and more!

BUTTON POETRY BEST SELLERS

Neil Hilborn, *Our Numbered Days*
Hanif Abdurraqib, *The Crown Ain't Worth Much*
Olivia Gatwood, *New American Best Friend*
Sabrina Benaim, *Depression & Other Magic Tricks*
Melissa Lozada-Oliva, *peluda*
Rudy Francisco, *Helium*
Rachel Wiley, *Nothing Is Okay*
Neil Hilborn, *The Future*
Phil Kaye, *Date & Time*
Andrea Gibson, *Lord of the Butterflies*
Blythe Baird, *If My Body Could Speak*
Rudy Francisco, *I'll Fly Away*
Andrea Gibson, *You Better Be Lightning*
Rudy Francisco, *Excuse Me As I Kiss The Sky*

Available at buttonpoetry.com/shop and more!